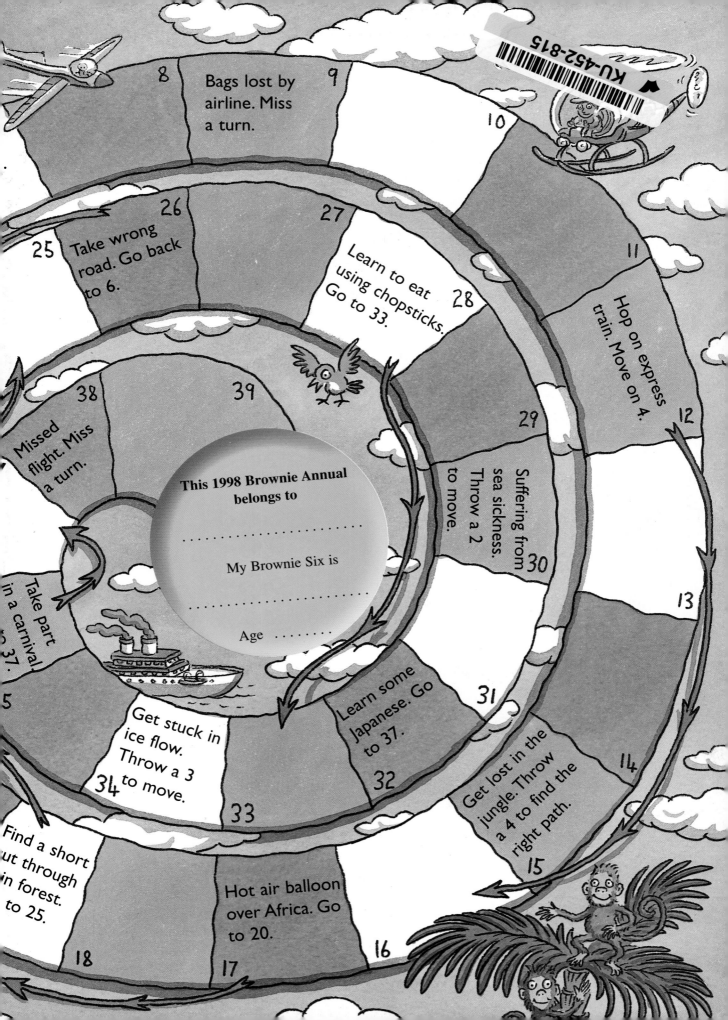

Brownie Guides

| Brownies are friendly | Brownies are wide awake | Brownies have fun out-of-doors | Brownies help at home | Brownies keep healthy | Brownies lend a hand | Brownies make things | Brownies do their best |

Brownies enjoy a balanced programme of activities covering eight points.

These symbols have been used in the 1998 *Brownie Annual* to show where activities fit in the Brownie Guide programme.

There is also a wide range of Interest Badges which Brownies can try that reflect the fun Brownies have at their meetings and at home. If an activity is linked to a badge it is shown on the page.

The full syllabuses for all Brownie Interest Badges can be found in the *Brownie Guide Badge Book*: the appropriate clauses for a badge must be fulfilled before a Brownie is entitled to wear it. This book is available from The Guide Association's trading outlets, ask your Brownie Guider for details.

Older Brownies can try the Go! Challenge. This symbol has been used to indicate an activity linked to the Go! Challenge.

Safety is always an issue when trying any activity. Some of the activities within this Annual require adult help or supervision.

THE GUIDE ASSOCIATION

Brownie Guides make a Promise. Freda, the pink elephant, helps Brownies remember their Promise. She can be found throughout this Annual giving helpful suggestions.

Brownie Annual

My Brownie Guide Promise

I promise that I will do my best:
To love my God,
To serve the Queen and my country,
To help other people
and
To keep the Brownie Guide Law.

The Brownie Guide Motto

Lend A Hand

The Brownie Guide Law

A Brownie Guide thinks of others before herself and does a Good Turn every day.

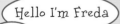
Hello I'm Freda

1998

Contents

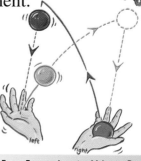

Paper Jewels, Going Batty, The Belly And The Members, Moving Pictures, The Heart At Work, Fancy Frames, Amazing Malaysia, Crazy Colours, The Story Of Cotton, Flying Skimmer, A Watery World, The Friendly Games, Snap Happy researched and written by John Malam: Creamy Snaps, Fruit Fizz, Viking Invaders recipes by Sandra Arnold: Strawberry Milkshake recipe by Andrea Hazeldine: Chocolate Crunch Cake recipe by Hilary Malam-Edwards: Fiery Food recipes by Sandra Arnold and Susan Jones: "But You Promised" written by Brenda Apsley. Thanks to: The Bat Conservation Trust (Going Batty): Action Images, for photographs kindly supplied, and The Football Association (Football Fans): Marina Dancy (Juggling): Girl Guides Association Malaysia (Amazing Malaysia): 8th West Finchley Brownie Pack (But You Promised): Lizzy Holton of the Rebel Stompers CWDC (Line Dancing): Marine Conservation Trust (A Watery World): 9th Andover Brownie Pack and St Ives (Andover) Ltd (Making A Magazine): Commonwealth Games Federation (The Friendly Games); Boots The Chemists Ltd (Snap Happy and Win A Camera!).

1998 Brownie Annual
© The Guide Association 1997

Going Batty photography © Frank Greenaway: Football Fans photography © Action Images and © TRIP Photographic Library: Focus on Fruit, Amazing Malaysia, The Story of Cotton, A Watery World, The Friendly Games photography © TRIP Photographic Library: The Heart At Work, illustration © George Turner: "Be Glad Your Nose Is On Your Face" © Jack Prelutsky appears in The New Kid On The Block by Jack Prelutsky, published by William Heinemann Ltd, it is reproduced here by permission of Reed Consumer Books: "The Cat With Blue Eyes" by John Grant, © Ladybird Books Ltd, illustration © Susan Hellard: "The Lobster Quadrille" by Lewis Carroll, illustration © George Turner: Win A Camera! photography © Boots The Chemists Ltd.

Published by The Guide Association, 17–19 Buckingham Palace Road, London SW1W 0PT: e-mail chq@guides.org.uk
An official publication of The Guide Association (incorporated by Royal Charter) registered charity number 306016
ISBN 0 85260 144 1
The Guide Association Trading Service ordering code 60053.

Brownie Guide Adviser Susan Jones: Project Editor Alice Forbes: Editor Clare Jefferis: Studio Manager Anne Moffat: Deputy Studio Manager Gillian Webb: Studio Marisa Escalant, David Jones, Caroline Marklew, Catherine Summers: Colour repro by Positive Colour Ltd: Printed and bound in Belgium by Proost NV.

Readers are reminded that during the life span of this publication policy changes may be made by The Guide Association which will affect the accuracy of information contained within these pages.

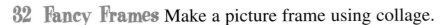

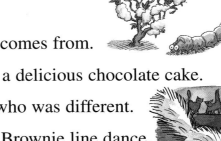

You'll find masses to choose from!

Paper Jewels

Why not design your own paper jewellery collection?

Papier mâché (said like 'pap-ee-yay mash-ay') is French for mashed paper. It is a mixture of paper and glue. When it dries it gets very hard. The Chinese made armour from it 2,000 years ago.

Papier mâché pulp

You will need
kitchen roll
or paper tissues
large mixing bowl
sieve
glue
plastic drinking straws
paints, felt-tip pens
or crayons
cotton thread,
string or wool

1 Tear the paper into small pieces, the smaller the better. Put about 4 mugfuls into the bowl. Cover with warm water. Soak for a few minutes.

2 Squeeze the paper to make a smooth pulp.

Glue recipe
Mix 3 tablespoons of plain white flour with 4 tablespoons of water. Stir well.

3 Pour the pulp into the sieve. Squeeze out the water. Put the pulp back in the bowl.

4 Add some glue. Mix so the pulp is sticky.

Illustrated by Adrian Barclay

Necklace

1 Take a small blob of papier mâché. Press it round a drinking straw to form a bead.

Wet papier mâché can be stored in a jar in the fridge. Stir again before using.

2 Make lots of other beads of different sizes. Papier mâché shrinks as it dries so make the beads larger than you want them to be.

3 Carefully remove the beads from the straw. Dry on a plate for several hours or overnight. For a quick dry, pop them in a warm oven or a microwave.

white

red

4 Decorate the beads. Paint them white, then pattern with bright colours.

5 Thread the beads onto the cotton.

Blue

Experiment with different shaped beads.

Going Batty

> Why are people scared of bats? Bats have a bad image because of the likes of Dracula, but they are beautiful and rare creatures

Bats need friends like you to help stop the number of bats in Britain declining.

Bats were once a common sight, especially at dusk. So why not now? Bats are nocturnal which means they sleep during the day, and come out at night. Each year there are fewer bats in this country. Why? Because their food is disappearing. Bats eat insects. Farmers and gardeners use chemicals to kill insects. Fewer insects means less food for bats.

Bats have large appetites. The pipistrelle bat can eat as many as 3,000 insects each night.

Many places where bats would roost have been destroyed. Old trees with holes have been felled. People visiting caves disturb and scare these timid animals.

Planting food

Insects which come out at night are important as this is when bats feed. Growing night-scented plants to attract these insects is one way of helping bats. Evening primroses tempt moths and other flying insects. Bats in the area may become regular night-time visitors.

Illustrated by Lisa Berkshire   Photographs © Frank Greenaway

Seeing in the dark?

As a bat flies it makes high-pitched sounds which travel from the bat like ripples on a pond. If an insect gets in the way these sound waves bounce back to the bat like an echo. By listening to the echo the bat knows exactly where the insect is. Our ears are not sensitive enough to be able to hear these sounds.

How you can help

To find out more about bats and how to join the Young Batworkers Club contact:
The Bat Conservation Trust
15 Cloisters House
8 Battersea Park Road
London SW8 4BG
Tel: 0171–627 2629
e-mail: batcontrust@gn.apc.org

Batty facts

Bats are mammals. They have fur and give birth to live young, like cats, dogs and horses. Bats are the only mammals that can fly. They can live for 30 years.

In 1991 the mouse-eared bat was declared extinct in Britain.

Britain's smallest bat is the pipistrelle. It is about four centimetres long and weighs about five grams, less than a two pence coin. Although it can fit into a match box its wings can stretch to 20 centimetres from tip to tip. It is often seen in towns.

Baby bats

Female bats usually have one baby each year during June or July. When it is born, a young bat doesn't have any fur and is blind. For the first few weeks it is dependent on its mother for milk. The mother hangs the baby in a safe place while she goes looking for food. By the autumn the baby has learnt to fly and catch its own insect food.

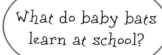

What do baby bats learn at school?

Hanging around

A bat hangs upside down in order to make it easier to take off for flying. It hangs by its feet but is able to climb around using its strong thumbs.

The alphabat!

11

Creamy Snaps

This yummy, creamy pudding has a cool crunch!

You will need
measuring jug
whisk
mixing bowl
serving dish
spoon
plastic food wrap

Ingredients
300 ml double cream
packet of ginger biscuits
150 ml orange juice

1 Whisk double cream. A hand whisk can be used instead of an electric one.

Invite a friend to share your creamy snaps.

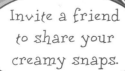

2 Dip biscuits into the orange juice. Do not let them get too soft! Place the dipped biscuits in a serving dish.

Illustrated by Martina Farrow

3 Cover the biscuits with some whipped cream.

4 Dip more biscuits in orange juice. Layer on top of the cream. Keep layering the cream and dipped biscuits. Finish with a layer of cream.

5 Cover with food wrap. Leave in fridge for 6 hours or overnight. Serve.

Ask an adult to show you how to use a whisk safely.

13

The Belly And

1 Once there was a Body. It was a very ordinary Body. It had many Members. Hands, Mouth, Teeth and Legs were all Members of this Body.

2 One day, the Members decided they were doing all the work. They said that while they worked hard, Belly got all the food.

3 The Members decided to stop working. They wanted Belly to do its fair share of work. Only then would they go back to work.

4 So, Hands stopped taking food. Mouth did not open. Teeth stopped biting. Legs sat down and refused to move Body.

Illustrated by Phil Garner

The Members

5 After two or three days, the Members wondered if they were doing the right thing. They all began to feel quite ill.

6 Hands began to tremble. Mouth felt thirsty. Teeth started to grind against each other. Legs felt weak and ached all the way to their toes.

7 Only then did the Members know that Belly was just as important as they were. In its own special way, Belly worked hard to keep Body fit.

8 The lesson to the Members was, "We must all work together." If the Members of the Body weren't a team, the Body would break down.

Football Fans

BROWNIE GUIDES

TRIP/PICTURESQUE

Kit and equipment

You need well-fitting and comfortable boots or trainers with a good grip. Shin pads are a good idea, too!

The Football World Cup is being held this summer in France. Brush up on your skills so you can enjoy the fun.

Dribbling

Learn to kick the ball in front of you as you run. Use the inside, outside and lace areas of both feet.

Did you know?

● Football was banned in medieval England because soldiers played football rather than practise archery.
● Americans call football 'soccer'.

ACTION IMAGES

Coaching and playing

For information on local coaching courses, teams and leagues to participate in contact:
- England 01707–651840
- Northern Ireland 01232–669458
- Scotland 0141–353 1162
- Wales 01222–372325

Passing

It is important to be able to pass the ball well to others in your team.

ACTION IMAGES

- Place your non-kicking foot beside the ball. Point this foot in the direction the ball is to go in.
- Check where the ball is going is clear.
- Concentrate on the ball.
- Kick the centre of the ball with a firm foot.
- Follow through in the direction the ball is going with your foot and leg.

Scoring a goal

When you have the chance – shoot for a goal!

ACTION IMAGES

- Place your non-kicking foot beside the ball.
- Keep your head still and over the ball.
- Kick the centre of the ball.
- Kick the ball using the laced area of your boot. Keep your ankle extended.
- Keep the ball low.

Your Six could form a football team.

Focus On

The pictures below are all different types of fruit. Can you work out what they are?

1

TRIP/R UNSWORTH

Apple

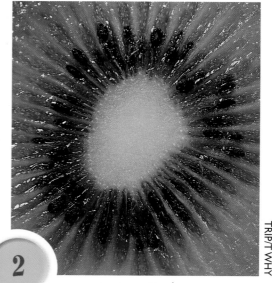

2

TRIP/T WHY

Kiwi fruit

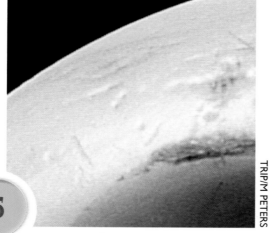

5

TRIP/M PETERS

bahna

6

TRIP/ANDY COLLISON

pineapple

Fruit

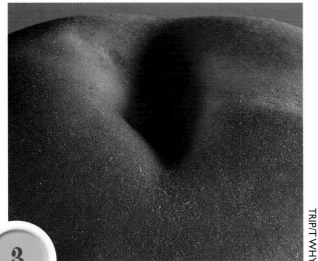

3

peach

TRIP/T WHY

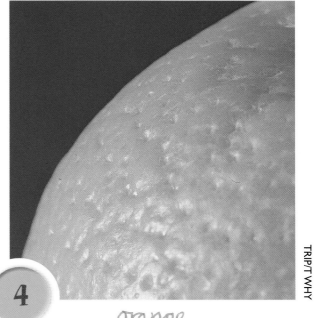

4

orange

TRIP/T WHY

7

cherry

TRIP/J & J WOOD

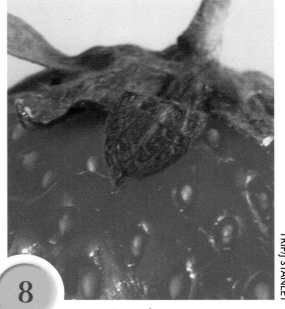

8

strawberry

TRIP/J STANLEY

See how well
you did!
Answers page 77.

Moving Pictures

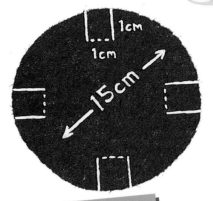

Imagine living 100 years ago – without television! Children played with zoetropes to see moving pictures. A zoetrope is a device which makes pictures appear to move. Have a go at making your own one.

1 Make a round base from thin black card as shown.

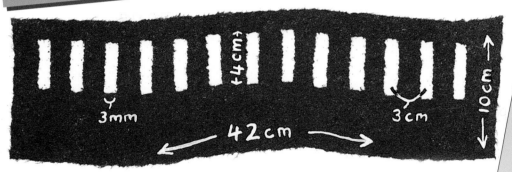

You will need
thin black card
plastic cap from aerosol can
large wire paper clip
sheet of white paper
modelling knife
felt-tip pens
sticky tape

2 Cut a strip of thin black card as shown. Sticky tape it to form a circle. Stick it to the round base.

Ask an adult to pierce the lid, and to show you how to use a knife safely.

3 Pierce a small hole in the can lid. Unbend one loop of the paper clip. Push it through the hole from underneath.

20

Illustrated by Frances Lloyd

4 On a strip of white paper draw a sequence showing various stages of someone or something moving. Make the drawings clear, simple and evenly spaced along the strip. Sticky tape it into a circle with the pictures inside.

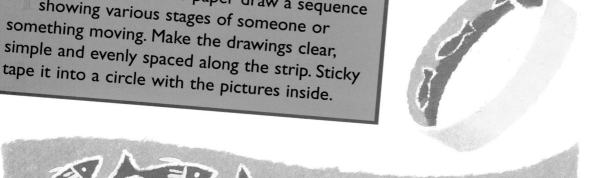

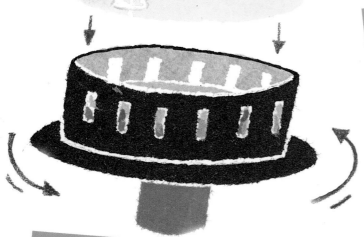

5 Slot the picture ring inside the black drum. Adjust it if necessary so it fits snugly. Place the drum on top of the paper clip spike.

6 Spin the zoetrope anticlockwise. Look through the slits. Do the pictures move?

Try different pictures.

How do they move?

The pictures move because your brain is confused. Your brain can't decipher quickly enough the first picture your eye sends it. It receives a second picture before it really understands the first. The pictures are so similar it appears to your brain that they are moving.

21

The Heart At

BROWNIE GUIDES

Your heart is like a little power station. All day, every day it pumps blood round your body. William Harvey discovered in 1628 how it all happens.

Your heart is like two strong pumps. There is one on the right side and one on the left.

The right pump sends the blood to your lungs.

● Blood carries oxygen and important nutrients to all the cells of your body. It also takes away waste produced by your cells.
● If all your blood vessels were placed end to end they would stretch two and a half times round the world.

In your lungs the blood picks up oxygen. The blood becomes very red. It goes back to your heart ready to travel round your body.

The artery divides. Some parts stretch up to your head. Others branch down your arms. The main part goes to organs like your liver and kidneys. It then divides so blood reaches each leg.

First the left pump sends it into a huge artery.

Illustrated by George Turner

Work

The blood needs to get back to your heart. The capillaries join to form small veins. All the veins from your head, arms, legs and main trunk eventually join together to form one big vein. This goes back into the right side of your heart so the blood can be pumped back to your lungs.

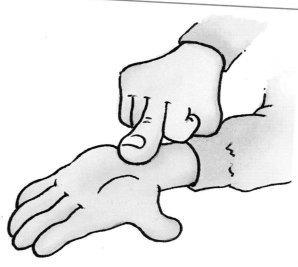

Use your middle finger to feel the pulse on your wrist. If you can't find the pulse, keep looking. It is there! How many times does your heart beat in a minute?

In the capillaries, the blood gives out oxygen and nutrients. The blood loses its redness. The capillaries start to get bigger.

Average pulse is about 70 beats per minute.

The arteries keep dividing to reach all parts of your body. Eventually they are so thin they are capillaries.

● Arteries take blood away from the heart.
● Veins take blood back to the heart.
● It takes about a minute for blood to get from your heart to your toes and back.

23

Cool Slurps

Feeling hot on a summer day? Cool yourself with these refreshing fruit slurps.

Fruit fizz

Something to bubble your taste buds.

You will need

measuring jug
mixing bowl
knife
chopping board
rolling pin
freezer bag
spoon

Ingredients

200 ml apple juice
200 ml orange juice
200 ml blackcurrant juice
apple
orange
600 ml lemonade
ice

1 Pour the apple juice, orange juice and blackcurrant juice into a bowl.

2 Cut the apple into quarters. Remove core. Slice thinly. Add to juice mixture. Peel the orange. Remove pith. Divide into segments. Chop the segments. Add to juice and apple mixture.

3 Place ice in freezer bag. Seal. Crush with rolling pin. Add to juice and fruit mixture. Add lemonade. Mix well. Serve.

Try making the milkshake with chocolate instead.

Illustrations by Lisa Berkshire

Strawberry milkshake

A gloopy, fruity smoothie.

You will need
measuring scales
food mixer
whisk
fork
mixing bowl
spoon or scoop

Ingredients
100 g strawberries
200 ml cold milk
large scoop vanilla
or strawberry
ice-cream

1 Wash the strawberries. Remove the leaves and stalks.

2 Mix everything in a food mixer, or use a whisk. Or mash strawberries with fork, whisk in milk, add ice-cream and whisk again. Serve.

Lemonade

This lemon drink has a real tangy zip!

1 Wash lemon. Dry. Grate peel into jug. Cut lemon in half. Squeeze juice from both halves. Add juice to grated peel.

You will need
fine grater
knife and chopping board
lemon squeezer
measuring jug
sieve
clean tea-towel
spoon and teaspoon

Ingredients
a lemon
teaspoon of honey

2 Mix in teaspoon of honey. Fill jug to 250 ml mark with boiling water. Mix well. Cover with cloth. Leave until cool. To serve, strain through sieve. Add ice.

Ask an adult to help you in the kitchen.

25

Be Glad Your Nose

Be glad your nose is on your face,
not pasted on some other place,
for if it were where it is not,
you might dislike your nose a lot.

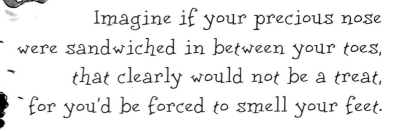

Imagine if your precious nose
were sandwiched in between your toes,
that clearly would not be a treat,
for you'd be forced to smell your feet.

Your nose would be a source of dread
were it attached atop your head,
it soon would drive you to despair,
forever tickled by your hair.

26

Illustrated by Jan Fearnley

Is On Your Face

Within your ear, your nose would be
an absolute catastrophe,
for when you were obliged to sneeze,
your brain would rattle from the breeze.

aa aaachoo !

Your nose, instead, through thick and thin,
remains between your eyes and chin,
not pasted on some other place –
be glad your nose is on your face!

Jack Prelutsky

'Be Glad Your Nose is On Your Face' appears in *The New Kid On The Block* by Jack Prelutsky, published by William Heinemann Ltd, reproduced here by permission of Reed Consumer Books.

Jugg

Impress your friends with some circus fun. Follow these easy steps to learn how to juggle.

BROWNIE GUIDES

You will need

3 juggling balls or bean bags
It's easier if each ball is a different colour. Balls need to fit snugly in your hands.

Prepare to juggle

Stand and face the edge of your bed. It stops you walking forward.

Check the area is clear of breakable objects – look above your head as well!

Baggy clothes can get in the way. Tie back long hair. Make sure your finger nails are short.

Stand with your feet slightly apart.

Now you are ready!

One at a time

1 Start with only one ball. Hold it in your right hand. Throw it up and to the left to reach about head height. When it gets to the top of the arc it should drop down. Catch it in your left hand.

2 Practise the same throw with your left hand. Catch it in your right hand. Repeat using each hand. Keep a steady rhythm.

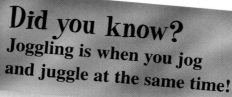

Did you know?
Joggling is when you jog and juggle at the same time!

Illustrated by Anna Hancock

ling

If you are left-handed you may want to swap right and left in these instructions.

3 Now try two balls. Hold one in each hand. Throw the one in your right hand as before. When it starts to drop, throw the ball in your left hand. Catch both balls. Practise the same throwing the ball in your left hand first. Repeat starting with the right hand, then the left.

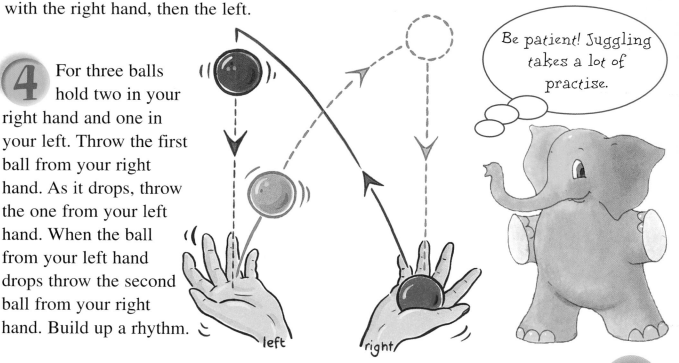

left   right

Top tips
● Look where you are throwing the ball.
● Don't look at your hands.
● Try to keep your hands at waist height.
● Try to stand still. Don't walk back or forward.

4 For three balls hold two in your right hand and one in your left. Throw the first ball from your right hand. As it drops, throw the one from your left hand. When the ball from your left hand drops throw the second ball from your right hand. Build up a rhythm.

left   right

Be patient! Juggling takes a lot of practise.

Green Games

Recycling is good for our planet. Less rubbish is buried in the ground. Fewer raw materials are used. Energy is saved. Less pollution goes into the atmosphere. What can you do to help? Find out with these puzzles.

Down which chute would you throw each piece of rubbish?

Illustrated by Derek Matthews

1 Worn by most people every day. You would be naked without them!
2 Grows on sheep. Can knit a jersey with it.
3 Where to put glass for recycling.
4 Natural fibre used for sewing.
5 Contains liquids, like milk. Can be made from glass or plastic.
6 Be careful with this. If it is broken it can cut you.
7 Thicker than paper. Makes strong boxes.
8 Gold, iron and copper are all this.
9 Read everyday to find out what has happened.
10 Carrier bags are made from this.
11 Buy baked beans in them. Need a special tool to open them.
12 Usually read weekly or monthly. *BROWNIE* is your favourite one!
13 Kitchen foil is made from this light metal.
14 Write on it. Made from trees.
15 A metal attracted by a magnet... that sounds like it is being stolen?

See how well you did! Answers page 77.

Fancy Frames

This fun, photo frame will make any picture look stunning.

Choose a photograph or picture you want to frame. It should be at least 10 cm by 15 cm.
Decide on the theme for the frame. Collect pictures from wrapping paper, magazines and cards. Cut them out.
Make sure none of them are larger than 6 cm.

You will need
2 pieces stiff card, 20 cm by 24 cm
pencil
ruler
scissors
felt-tip pens, crayons (not wax) or paints
pictures
paper glue
sticky tape

1 Carefully cut a rectangle from one piece of card. Keep the rectangle safe. Rejoin the corner at the back.

2 Decorate the frame. Paint or colour it first if you want. Cut out the pictures.

3 Arrange the pictures before gluing. Place the frame over the photograph to check nothing important is being hidden. Glue the pictures in place.

What is collage?
Collage is a French word meaning 'gluing' or 'pasting'. It is a method of pasting paper and other materials to make a picture.

32

Illustrated by Adrian Barclay

4 Tape the photograph in position. Glue the second piece of card to the back.

Glue

5 Fold the rectangle of card in half twice. Cut the middle two thicknesses only.

6 Tape the stand to the back.

Find out about photography on page 72.

33

Amazing

The 16th Commonwealth Games will be held this summer in West Malaysia.

Houses

Malay villages are called kampungs. Traditional kampung houses are made from bamboo or wood and have thatched roofs.

Tropical houses are built on stilts to raise them above the damp ground.

Sarawak, is famous for longhouses. A longhouse is like a village as everyone lives in one building. Families have separate rooms and share a veranda.

Weather

Malaysia is hot all year round. The weather is tropical and there are monsoons each year. About 2.5 metres of rain fall each year!

Land

Malaysia has many mountains. It is also covered in tropical rainforests and mangrove swamps. Near the sea the land is flatter. Stretching down the coast are long, sandy beaches.

TRIP/W JACOBS

TRIP/A GASSON

Flag

The strips represent the 13 Malaysian states and the capital. The crescent and star are symbols of Islam. The blue reminds people of their link with Britain.

Illustrated by Sue Faulks

Malaysia

Animals

Malaysia has many unusual animals, such as the tapir and pangolin. The pangolin is a scaly anteater that can grow up to a metre long. It is nocturnal and lives in the forest. Other Malaysian animals include the water buffalo, mongoose, orangutan, tiger and black panther.

Fact file

Capital: Kuala Lumpur
Highest mountain: Mount Kinabalu (4,101 metres)
Population: 19.5 million
Official language: Bahasa Malaysia
Religions: Islam, Buddhism, Taoism, Hinduism, Christianity
Money: Malay dollar (ringgit) = 100 cents (sen)
Main products: tin, rubber, palm oil, timber, chemicals, electronic goods

Language

In Bahasa Malaysia:
'selamat pagi' means 'good morning.'
'selamat jalan' means 'goodbye.'

Festivals

Every July and August in Penang there are dragon boat races as part of a festival. According to legend, local fishermen paddled out to save a Chinese saint who was drowning. They beat their drums to scare away the fish.

Motto

Lend a hand

Brownies

Brownies in Malaysia are called Tunas Puteri which means 'shoots that will grow into useful plants if carefully looked after.' Tunas Puteri are aged between six and 12 years old. They wear a white blouse, brown skirt and a scarf.

Promise

I promise to do my best
To do my duty to God, the King and my country Malaysia.
To help other people every day especially at home.
To obey the Brownie Laws.

Try your own Commonwealth Games on page 66.

Laws

A Brownie gives in to older folks.
A Brownie does not give in to herself.

Viking Invaders

About a thousand years ago sea warriors raided and settled all across Europe, including the United Kingdom. They mainly came from Norway and were called Vikings. They sailed across the North Sea in long boats.

These long boats are fun to make – and can be eaten as well!

You will need
large plate
baking foil
sharp knife
chopping board
knife
cocktail sticks

Ingredients
3 'hot dog' finger rolls
butter or margarine
3 cheese slices
3 slices cooked meat
tomatoes
cucumber

1 Cover the plate with foil to make the sea.

2 Cut bread rolls in half. Spread with butter or margarine.

Why not visit the Jorvik Viking Centre?

Call York's Jorvic Viking Centre information hotline 01904-653000 for admission details. Check with the person who pays the bill before using the phone.

3 Make shields. Slice tomatoes and cucumber. Pierce roll with cocktail stick. Attach slice of tomato or cucumber to either end. Continue until all rolls have shields along full length.

36

Illustrated by Frances Lloyd

4 Make sails. Push cocktail stick through corners of meat or cheese slice. Position in centre of long boat.

5 Position on sea. Serve.

Ask an adult to show you how to use a knife safely.

37

But You Promised!

New neighbours were moving in next to Jo...

I've come to say hi. My name's Jo.

I'm Hayley.

They were soon chatting like friends.

You'll love school. Monday is netball, Tuesday aerobics and Thursday's Brownies.

Hayley met some of Jo's friends.

Brownies?! You are joking? Brownies is f[or] sad people. No way!

Jo and Hayley spent all their free time together. They liked the same music, clothes, posters... even the same boys! But Hayley didn't go to Brownies.

Gita and Jo always walked to Brownies together, but one Thursday...

I'm not coming to Brownies tonight.

Brownies is for babies.

What do you know about Brownies? You've never been!

On Saturday afternoon...

Wow! A new rollerblading rink! It's opening tonight. Let's go. I can wear the new shorts Mum's promised me.

Photographs by Diana Aynaci

Staying Alive

Would you know how to survive in a car stuck in a snowdrift? How can you make sure water is safe to drink?

Water

Water must be safe to drink. One way of doing this is to make a solar still.

Plastic.

Seal edge of plastic.

Dig a small hole.

Clean container.

Water in the ground evaporates and small droplets form on the plastic. The droplets will fall into the container. Make sure animals and insects don't drink the water before you!

It is rarely safe to drink water from streams and rivers.

Street wise

Being safe on the streets is important. Do you know the Green Cross Code? Use it every time you cross a road.

Don't accept lifts from strangers.

Avoiding dangerous situations is important. Talk with an adult about safety and survival.

Find out about bus and train times and fares.

40

Illustrated by Anna Hancock

Car journey

What action should be taken if you and your family got stuck in a snow drift?

It is always wise to make sure there is a survival kit in the car. Remember to include items in case the car breaks down, as well as things to keep you warm. A bottle of water and a first aid kit are vital too.

- Switch off the engine.
- Don't run the engine too often.
- Check exhaust is clear.
- Shelter in the car, rescuers will find you more easily.
- Tie something bright to the top of the car or the aerial so you are easier to spot.
- Open a window a little. If the snow gets really deep push an air hole through it.

Make sure an adult knows where you are, who you are with and what time you will be home. Let them know if your plans change.

Keep to well-lit and busy areas.

Think ahead. Be prepared!

Sit downstairs near the front of the bus.

Sit in a busy carriage on a train. If the carriage empties move to a busier carriage. Know where the emergency cord is.

Cryptic Clothing

What do you know about the clothes on your back? Find out with these puzzles.

What do these symbols mean? Draw the symbol in the box beside its meaning.

hand wash

warm iron

wash at 40° C

dry clean

do not tumble dry

Where do the following come from? Link the material or fabric on the left with its source on the right.

sheep

goat

rabbit

alpaca

angora

cashmere

wool

silk

cotton

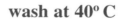

Illustrated by Dom Mansell

Can you find the following words in the word-hex? The letters for each word are next to one another, but can zig-zag about. The last letter of one word is the first letter of the next. The puzzle starts and ends on the A.

BROWNIE GUIDES

acrylic
batik
care label
cloth
elastic
garment
hand washing
knit
laundry
needle
nylon
taffeta
twin tub
yarn

bush

worm

llama

See how well
you did!
Answers
page 77.

Crazy Colours

Tie dyeing is fun, colourful and very, very messy! Take that old, tired T-shirt and give it fresh life. Create a new wardrobe. Dazzle your friends!

BROWNIE GUIDES

Dye will stain everything it touches – be careful! Ask an adult to show you how to use an iron safely.

What is tie dyeing?

It is an ancient technique for colouring clothes. By tying fabric in special ways and soaking it in dye you can create colourful, crazy patterns. Each one is unique!

Dyes can be bought in hardware stores and fabric shops. Check that it is suitable for cotton and it is a cold water dye. Dyes might not work on patterned materials or fabrics that have already been dyed.

1 Wet the T-shirt so it is damp. Pinch a small clump. Wind string round the base. Tighten the string and knot. Rubber bands can be used instead of string. Repeat all over.

DYE

2 Fill the bowl with enough water to cover the T-shirt. Make up the dye following the packet instructions. Stir well. Pour into the bowl of water.

Illustrated by Adrian Barclay

3 Dissolve the salt and cold dye fix in very hot tap water following the packet instructions. Add to the bowl.

4 Put the T-shirt in the water. Don't fold or crease. Stir for 10 minutes. Leave for 50 minutes stirring occasionally.

5 Remove from the bowl. Rinse until the water runs clear. Untie the string. Wash, dry, then iron before wearing.

Try dyeing a pair of leggings or a hanky!

Experiment with natural dyes like beetroot or onion.

Other patterns

● For circles, pull a long clump from the centre. Tie in several places.

● Make swirls in the same way as circles, but twist as you tie. Check it doesn't untwist after tying.

● Also try pleating from top to bottom. Tie in several places.

The Story Of

Did you know your favourite cotton T-shirt started life growing on a bush? This is its story.

Cotton is grown in more than 70 countries round the world. It grows best in warm and hot climates. China grows more than a quarter of the world's cotton. The USA, Russia, India, Pakistan, Brazil, Turkey and Egypt are also important cotton-growing countries.

TRIP/J WAKELIN

Cotton fields

Cotton plants grow in fields like wheat and other crops. They grow up to two metres tall and have large leaves with lots of funnel-shaped flowers. The flowers' white, yellow or reddish petals become pink, then purple after a few days.

The flowers turn into seed pods called bolls. Each boll is packed with about 50 seeds each covered in fine, creamy-white cotton fibres. Up to half a million fibres can grow inside each boll. The cotton fibres thicken and grow two to six centimetres long. Once the fibres have dried in the sun they can be harvested.

The cotton bolls are hand plucked from the plants by teams of cotton pickers, or they are stripped off using a huge harvesting machine.

Illustration by Dom Mansell

Cotton

Making yarn

The dry bolls are put through a machine called a 'gin' which removes the fibres from the seeds. The fibres are gathered up and pressed into huge bales that are sold to a cotton mill.

At the cotton mill the millions of tiny fibres are joined together to make yarn. The machine used to do this is called a spinning frame. The yarn looks like a very long piece of strong, white string.

TRIP/H ROGERS

The cotton seeds left when the fibres are removed from the bolls are not wasted. They are split open. The shells are used for cattle food. The insides are squeezed and the oil which comes out goes into margarine, cosmetics, soap and paint.

TRIP/F TORRANCE

Fabricating clothes

The yarn can then be used to make cotton fabrics. Machines are used to knit or weave the yarn into pieces of material.

All cotton at this stage is white. It can now be dyed or printed. Once this has been done, the fabric can be used to make clothes.

TRIP/H ROGERS

Page 44 has a fab idea for cotton T-shirts!

Chocolate

This colourful, choccy cake is just the thing to get your teeth into!

You will need
measuring scales
mixing bowl
tablespoon
dessertspoon
teaspoon
saucepan (optional)
loaf tin or similar
plastic food wrap
knife

Ingredients
200 g milk chocolate
1½ tablespoons syrup
1 dessertspoon soft margarine
250 g red, green and yellow glacé cherries
2 digestive biscuits
2 dessertspoons puffed rice cereal
1 teaspoon chopped glacé ginger

1 Break chocolate into pieces. Place in bowl. Melt chocolate in microwave oven*. Heat for 30 seconds. Remove. Stir. Heat for further 30 seconds. Remove. Stir. Heat for further 15 seconds. Alternatively, melt chocolate in bowl over pan of boiling water.

Don't eat too many at once!

*Times given are for D rating/800 watt microwave oven. Adjust times according to power of oven.

Illustrated by Martina Farrow

Crunch Cake

2 Add syrup. Mix. Add margarine. Mix. Break biscuits into small pieces. Add and mix. Add cherries, rice cereal and ginger. Mix well. Warm mixture in microwave oven for 15 seconds if too stiff.

3 Line loaf tin. Spoon mixture into loaf tin. Press mixture down so there are no spaces. Leave to cool.

4 Place in fridge for two hours to set.

5 Turn out cake onto plate. Remove plastic food wrap. Cut into 1 cm fingers. Serve.

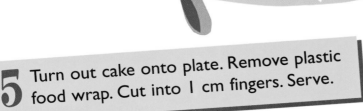

Ask an adult to show you how to use a microwave oven safely.

49

The Cat With Blue Eyes

On fine nights the cats sat on the back fence. There were five of them, and their leader was Nelson, who only had one eye. They talked about this and that. Some-times they had a sing-song. Anyone looking out after dark would see a row of nine green eyes.

So there was quite a stir on the back fence when a new cat arrived. All the others were black or tabby. Julius, the new cat, was a grubby white. His fur was very long and untidy. It hung down over his face, with just the tip of his nose and his ears showing. He was homeless, and Nelson made him welcome. He turned out to be a good singer. And he had a lot to talk about.

50

Written by John Grant, © Ladybird Books Ltd.   Illustrated by Susan Hellard

One night, Nelson had problems with some particularly troublesome mice. So, it was quite late when he arrived at the back fence to see eight green eyes in a row… and two BLUE! It was Julius. The evening breeze had blown the fur back off his face, and they all saw his eyes for the first time. None of them had ever seen BLUE eyes before!

"He's different!" cried the cats. "A troublemaker," cried Nelson. They chased Julius away from the back fence… and told him not to come back!

Julius was very unhappy. He was also hungry. He curled up in a corner of the churchyard to sleep. In the morning he went to rummage in a handy dustbin for something to eat. Suddenly a voice croaked, "Good morning. You're new around here." It was a cheeky looking jackdaw.

Julius told him his troubles. "Hang on," said the jackdaw. It flew up to its nest, which was full of bright, shiny things that jackdaws like to steal. A moment later, the jackdaw fluttered down beside Julius with a pair of green-tinted sun glasses. Julius tried them on. "Cool, man!" croaked the jackdaw.

Julius set off that evening to join the cats on the back fence. Cats can usually see in the dark – but not when they are wearing dark glasses. Julius leapt up, missed his footing, and fell over the other side. The other cats all laughed.

Julius slunk away. It began to rain. Tired, wet and hungry, he was sitting by the roadside when a lady drove past. She stopped, picked Julius up, and took him home.

Once he was fed, dry and combed, Julius looked quite different. A neighbour looked in. "What a beautiful cat!" she cried. "He's a long-haired British white! And, those eyes! You have a champion here!"

And she was right. The kind lady entered Julius for a cat show, where he won all the prizes. He was a star! He acted on television, advertising cat food. When he made a personal appearance in the local supermarkets, the cats from the back fence went to see him. And Julius was really very nice to them. He made sure that they all got samples of the cat food he was advertising.

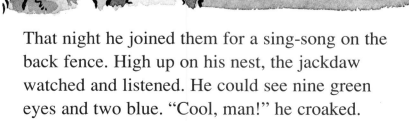

That night he joined them for a sing-song on the back fence. High up on his nest, the jackdaw watched and listened. He could see nine green eyes and two blue. "Cool, man!" he croaked.

Reprinted by permission of Ladybird Books

Line Dancing

Line dancing started in the United States of America. The dancers form rows of lines and dance the same steps together. As well as keeping you fit it is great fun.

Walls

At the start of the dance you face the first 'wall'. After doing the steps once you face a different direction, the second wall. There are usually four walls altogether. Repeat the steps until the music ends, each time facing a different wall.

The zoom dance

This special Brownie line dance has two walls. You need American country music with slow or medium beat. Get used to it by tapping to the beat with your toe.

Learn the steps without the music. When you know them well do each move to a beat of the music.

whoopee!

Yee ha!

Don't forget to smile.

Line dancers look really spectacular in their bright shirts, cowboy hats, jeans and boots.

BROWNIE GUIDES

54

Illustrated by Anna Hancock

Start the Zoom dance with your feet together.

Right strut

1 Step on right heel.

2 Bring down right toe.

Left strut

3 Step on left heel.

4 Bring down left toe.

Right strut

5 Step on right heel.

6 Bring down right toe.

Left strut

7 Step on left heel.

8 Bring down left toe.

9 Step back on right foot.

10 Step back on left foot.

11 Step back on right foot.

12 Stomp left foot beside right foot.

13 Step right foot to right.

14 Step left foot beside right foot.

15 Step right foot to right.

16 Step left foot to touch right foot.

17 Step left foot to left.

18 Step right foot beside left foot.

19 Step left foot to left.

20 Stomp right foot beside left foot.

Right fan

21 Turn right toe to right (heel stays in place).

22 Turn right toe back beside left foot.

Left fan

23 Turn left toe to left (heel stays in place).

24 Turn left toe back beside right foot.

25 Left foot ¼ turn to left.

26 Stomp right foot beside left foot.

27 Left foot ¼ turn to left.

28 Stomp right foot beside left foot.

Start the Zoom dance again!

Choreographed by Lizzy Holton

55

Fire Fighting

Knowing how to cope if there was a fire is important. Test your skills with these puzzles.

What would you do or check to make this kitchen safer, or even prevent a fire?

1.................................... 2 ....

3.................................... 4 ....

5.................................... 6 ....

Illustrated by Derek Matthews

Can you find the following words in the square below?

alarm   axe   burns   detector   emergency   engine

extinguisher   fire   fire officer   fire station   flames   fuel

heat   helmet   hose   hydrant   mask   match

oxygen   sirens   smoke   sparks   water

```
F B D E T E C T O R M E
I T S N R U B H C T A M
R A P G S Z L S H W H E
E X T I N G U I S H E R
S E N N A L A R M O A G
T U A E F E K E O S T E
A K R X D U I N K E F N
T S D E B F C S E B L C
I A Y F H E L M E T A Y
O M H I N E G Y X O M N
N F I R E O F F I C E R
W A T E R S K R A P S D
```

See how well you did! Answers page 77.

55

Flying Skimmer

This amazing paper 'aeroplane' is easy to make and fun to fly. Build your own and see how far it will go.

The skimmer is made using origami, the ancient Japanese art of paper folding. Paper has always been important to the Japanese. It was used to make windows in their houses, and also umbrellas.

You will need
8 squares of strong paper, 5 cm by 5 cm
sticky tape
scissors

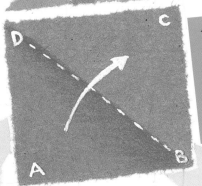

1 Fold each square in half from A to C.

2 Fold each triangle from B to A.

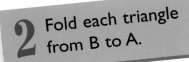

Illustrated by Frances Lloyd

Beat this

● The world's biggest paper aeroplane had a wingspan of 9.15 metres.

● The current world record for flying a paper aeroplane indoors is 18.8 seconds.

3 Place point D of one piece into the pocket of another piece.

4 Continue until all pieces join to form a ring.

5 Turn the ring over. Fold each C as shown.

6 Stick the pieces together with sticky tape.

Try making it with different sized squares.

Flying lessons

Hold the ring between your thumb and index finger. Hold it close to your chest. Flick it quickly from the wrist, then the elbow like a Frisbee. How far will it fly?

A Watery W

A Watery W

This year is the International Year of the Ocean. How much do you know about oceans?

Ocean facts

● The largest ocean is the Pacific. It contains over half the world's water. It is bigger than all the world's land put together.

● More than half the oxygen we breathe is made by algae in the world's oceans and seas.

● Salt from the world's oceans and seas could cover all the land in a layer 150 metres deep.

● The Marianas Trench, a huge valley at the bottom of the Pacific Ocean, is the world's deepest point. A stone would take an hour to fall to the bottom!

To find out more about the world's oceans contact:
Marine Conservation Society
9 Gloucester Road
Ross-on-Wye
Herefordshire HR9 5BU
(send an SAE)
Tel: 01989–566017
e-mail: mcsuk@gn.apc.org

TRIP/J GARRETT

MARINE CONSERVATION SOCIETY

rld

Every day...

...more than 5,000,000 items of waste are thrown into the oceans and seas by ships.

...1,000 dolphins and 3,000 sharks are caught and left to die in fishing nets.

...300 marine mammals and 3,000 seabirds die from pollution in the sea.

TRIP/AUSTRALIAN PIC LIB

There are five oceans:
- Arctic Ocean.
- Atlantic Ocean.
- Indian Ocean.
- Pacific Ocean.
- Southern Ocean.

TRIP/AUSTRALIAN PIC LIB

Great Barrier Reef

Coral is the limestone skeletons of tiny sea animals called polyps. When they die their skeletons remain. A coral reef is made from billions and billions of these tiny limestone skeletons.

The Great Barrier Reef is the world's longest coral reef and is just north east of Australia. It is a series of small coral islands that stretch for more than 2,000 kilometres.

More than 5,000 different species of animals and plants live on the Great Barrier Reef. Colourful fish, fan-like corals, delicate sea anemones and sponges are just some of the reef's inhabitants.

World Oceans Day is on 8 June 1998.

Fiery Food

Dazzle your friends at Pack Holiday with these fabulous cook out ideas. Ask an adult to help you try them.

Kebabs

Chop onions, mushrooms, peppers, courgettes, aubergines and tomatoes into small pieces. Push them onto a skewer. Place over the fire. Turn them frequently. Take care the skewer can get very hot! Remove from the skewer before eating. Fruit kebabs using different chopped fruits are tasty too.

Sausage sizzle

Lay the sausages in a shallow frying pan. Prick them with a fork. Place over the fire. Turn frequently. Before serving, cut one in half to make sure the middle is cooked.

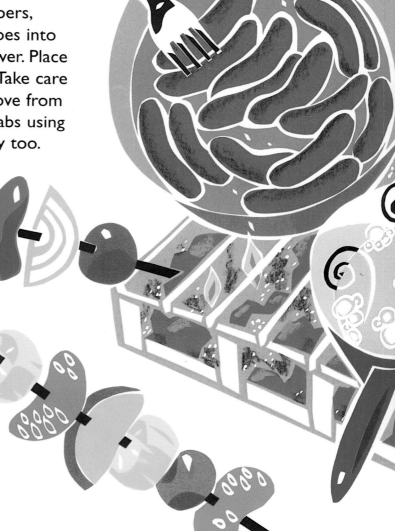

If you can't cook these on a fire grill the kebabs, cook the bananas in an oven, fry or grill the sausages heat the milk on a cooker.

⚠ Never light or cook on a fire without adult help.

⚠ Burns should be immersed immediately in cold water.

⚠ A fire can be put out with sand, or by sprinkling it with water.

62

Illustrated by Martina Farrow

Mallow chocolate

Measure a mug of milk into a pan. Place over the fire. Empty a sachet of chocolate drink powder into the mug. Pour the boiling milk into the mug. Stir well. Drop a marshmallow on top. Sip through the melted marshmallow.

Banana squidge

Slit a banana lengthways. Stuff with chunks of chocolate. Wrap in baking foil. Scrunch the foil edges over so they are sealed. Place in the embers. Cook for about 10 minutes. Remove from embers. Open foil. Eat with a spoon.

Fires can be dangerous. Ask an adult to help you with this activity.

Making A Magazine

BROWNIE is the brilliant magazine for Brownie Guides packed with puzzles, stories, competitions, things to make as well as news about other Brownies.

Brownies from all over Britain write to the magazine. Some of their letters appear on *BROWNIE*'s 'Pinboard' pages.

The editor reads all the letters then decides which ones to print. She carefully keys each letter on to her computer making sure there are no spelling mistakes and shortening long letters. The editor organises and writes about the prizes and special offers for 'Pinboard'. She sends her computer file of the words to the designer.

BROWNIE facts
Each year...
- 11,000,000 pages are printed.
- 31 tonnes of paper are used reaching 600 kilometres, that's about the same distance between Edinburgh and London.
- 1.25 tonnes of ink are used, about the same weight as 10 baby elephants.

Photographs by Diana Aynaci

Cut out and colour in
your special Brownie
Annual bookmark

Brownie annual 1998

BOOKMARK

Brownie magazine

Have you ever seen *BROWNIE* magazine? It's full of puzzles, stories, recipes, things to make, fascinating facts, and news about other Brownies.

If you would like to receive your own copy of the magazine every month, please fill in your details here.

Please send me a subscription form for *BROWNIE* magazine.

Name ....

Pack ....

Address ....

....

.... Postcode ....

2

Publishing Services (BA)
FREEPOST (LON 145)
The Guide Association
LONDON
SW1W 0YA

One of *BROWNIE*'s three designers puts the words and pictures on her computer. The designer uses special computer software to move the words and pictures around until they look good and all fit on to the pages.

Next the editor carefully checks that nothing has been missed off, and the right words are with the right pictures. This final computer file is saved on a disk and sent to the repro house where it is turned into film.

This photographic film is the same size as the magazine page. The repro house makes a colour proof from the film for the designer and editor to check.

BROWNIE facts
● Work on the January issue of *BROWNIE* starts in October to make sure it is ready in time.
● At any one time, editors, designers and printers can be working on up to four issues of *BROWNIE* – that's 128 pages!

The film is sent to the printers to be made into printing plates on thin sheets of metal. Next the plates for 'Pinboard' and the rest of the magazine are loaded on to a huge printing press. *BROWNIE* is then printed on to a reel of paper. The printer makes sure the paper is cut and folded in a special way so the pages appear in the right order. *BROWNIE* is then stapled together and bundled up.

BROWNIE magazine
The Guide Association
17-19 Buckingham Palace Road
London SW1W 0PT
e-mail: chq@guides.org.uk

Have you ever written to *BROWNIE* magazine? Maybe your letter will appear in 'Pinboard.' Each month *BROWNIE* has a special prize for the star letter.

Finally copies of *BROWNIE* are delivered to the newsagents, shops and supermarkets ready for you to buy.

The Friendly Games

TRIP/R CHESTER

The Friendly Games is another name for the Commonwealth Games. Every four years sportswomen and men compete at this event. In 1998 the Games are being held in Malaysia.

Hold your own Friendly Games by trying these events.

BROWNIE GUIDES
BROWNIE GUIDES
BROWNIE GUIDES

Baked bean bowls

Place an unopened tin of baked beans at one end of the room. Gently roll a small ball towards it. How close to the tin can you get it? Challenge a friend to do better. The trick is to knock your opponent's ball away from the tin and get yours closer.

Jump!
How high can you jump?

Illustrated by Sue Faulks

Gymnastics

Pick your favourite piece of music. Create a routine which gently stretches your legs, arms and tummy. Use flowing ribbons to make it more spectacular.

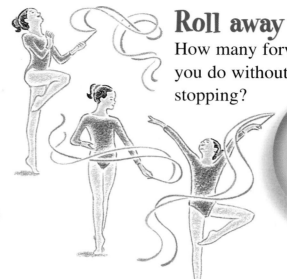

Roll away

How many forward rolls can you do without stopping?

How many backward rolls can you manage?

Jump!

How far can you jump?

Cricket

Make a bat from rolled up newspaper. Use empty, plastic bottles for wickets. With a friend take turns to bat and bowl. Who can score the most runs?

Find out about Malaysia on page 34.

The beam

Upturn some sturdy (and empty) flowerpots. Place them one pace apart. Can you walk from one end to the other without falling off?

Puzzle Corner

Dotty problem
Stare at the squares for a minute. Do you see black spots where the white lines join?

Quickly!
Ask your friend to mark the middle of a square of paper with a cross. Then ask her to rip it into nine pieces as shown. Ask her to then jumble the pieces so you can't see the mark. Can you find the marked piece immediately?

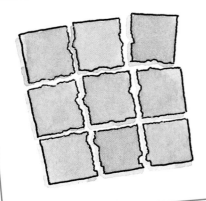

Meaningful words
What are these trying to say?

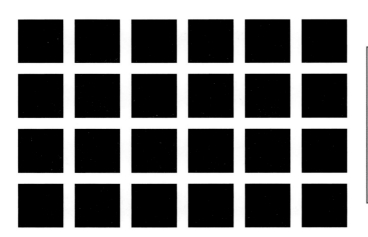

Calculator
Multiply 205128 by 4. Then divide it by 4. Keep multiplying it and dividing it quickly. Watch the 8 leap from the end to the front.

Illustrated by Phil Garner

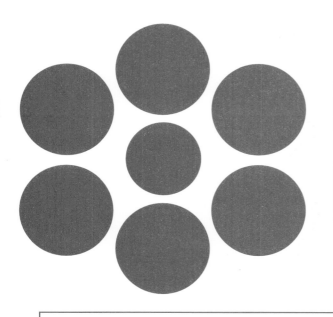

Eye test
Which of the two centre circles is larger?

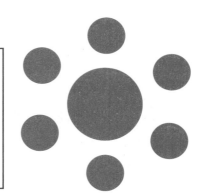

Drink time
Can you work out what these drinks are?

NLIAVAL LAKKHMEIS

DOLMEENA

GAONER CJEIU

CEI-MACER DAOS

LCAO

See how well you did! Answers page 77.

I is...
Miss Rite asked her class to say a sentence starting with "I".
"I am eight," said Lisa.
"Good," said Miss Rite.
"I is…," started Louise.
"No," interrupted Miss Rite, "always start with 'I am…'."
"I am the ninth letter of the alphabet," continued Louise.

The truth
Amy can't lie. Angela never tells the truth. One of them said, "She says she is Angela." Was it Amy or Angela who said this?

The Lobster

"Will you walk a little faster?" said a
whiting to a snail.
"There's a porpoise close behind us,
and he's treading on my tail.
See how eagerly the lobsters and the
turtles all advance!
They are waiting on the shingle –
will you come and join the dance?
Will you, won't you, will you, won't
you, will you join the dance?
Will you, won't you, will you, won't
you, won't you join the dance?

"You can really have no notion how
delightful it will be,
When they take us up and throw us,
with the lobsters, out to sea!"
But the snail replied "Too far, too
far!" and gave a look askance –
Said he thanked the whiting kindly,
but he would not join the dance.
Would not, could not, would not, could
not, would not join the dance.
Would not, could not, would not, could
not, could not join the dance.

Illustrated by George Turner

Quadrille

"What matters it how far we go?" his
scaly friend replied.
"There is another shore, you know,
upon the other side.
The further off from England the
nearer is to France –
Then turn not pale, beloved snail,
but come and join the dance.
Will you, won't you, will you, won't
you, will you join the dance?
Will you, won't you, will you, won't
you, won't you join the dance?"

Lewis Carroll

Lewis Carroll lived from 1832 to 1898.
His real name was Charles Lutwidge
Dodgson. He is best known for writing
Alice's Adventures in Wonderland and
Through The Looking Glass. Charles
Dodgson also taught mathematics at
Oxford University, and Alice Liddell
was the middle daughter of the dean. It
was during a boating trip on 4 July
1862 that Charles Dodgson invented
the story of Alice's underground
adventures.

Snap Happy

Photographs are a brilliant way of remembering the exciting things you have done.

Taking photographs

- Use both hands.
- Keep your elbows close to your body.
- Hold the camera lightly against your nose.
- Keep your fingers, hair and camera strap away from the lens.
- Take a deep breath just before taking a photograph. Breathe out after pressing the shutter release button.
- Hold the camera steady. Pressing the shutter release button too hard can make the camera shake.

Make the fun photo frame on page 32.

- 'Frame' the picture in the viewfinder.
- Move backwards or forwards to make the picture fit. Look behind you before stepping back.
- Turn the camera if the picture is long and thin.

Illustrated by Anna Hancock

Cameras

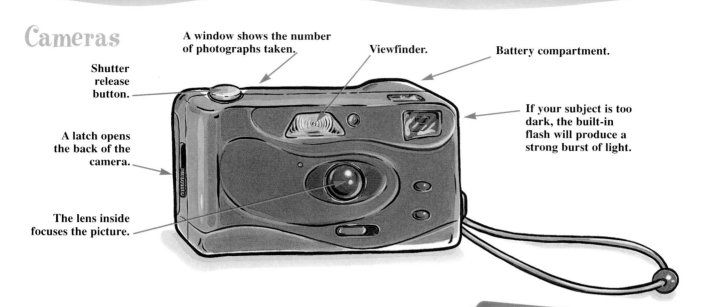

A window shows the number of photographs taken.

Viewfinder.

Battery compartment.

Shutter release button.

A latch opens the back of the camera.

The lens inside focuses the picture.

If your subject is too dark, the built-in flash will produce a strong burst of light.

Through the pinhole

Here's a chance to make your own camera. This pinhole camera doesn't take photographs but you can see how the image is formed.

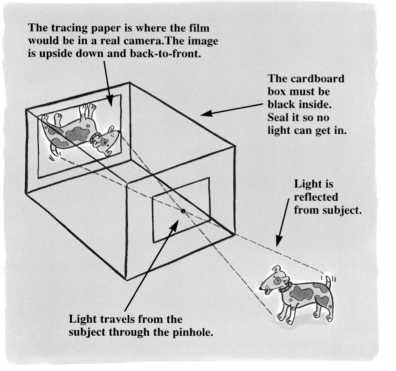

The tracing paper is where the film would be in a real camera. The image is upside down and back-to-front.

The cardboard box must be black inside. Seal it so no light can get in.

Light is reflected from subject.

Light travels from the subject through the pinhole.

For best results a pinhole camera must be light-tight. The brighter the subject, the better the image.

Do's and don'ts

- Do keep the camera in its case.
- Do check how much film is left.
- Do make sure the battery still works.
- Don't open the back of the camera unless you need to put in a new film, or take out a used film.
- Don't touch the lens.
- Don't let the camera get wet, hot or muddy. Avoid getting sand in it.

Win a super camera! Turn to the next page.

Win A Ca

Think of all the fun you could have with a camera. Try your photographer badge. Have fun with your friends snapping the action!

What to do

1 Draw a picture of what you would photograph if you won the camera. It must show an exciting thing you have done as a Brownie.

It could be:
- **what you do with your Six.**
- **the fun you have at Pack Holiday.**
- **what you did for a badge.**
- **the games you play at meetings.**

Brownie Annual has 10 super camera prizes for the great 1998 competition.

2 Write on the back of your drawing:
- **what you like best about Brownies.**
- **your favourite three things from this Annual.**
- **how many times Freda appears in the 1998 *Brownie Annual*.**
- **your name.**
- **your age.**
- **your address.**

3 Carefully put your entry in an envelope and send it to:

Win A Camera!
1998 Brownie Annual
Competition
The Guide Association
17–19 Buckingham Palace Road
London SW1W 0PT

Don't forget the stamp!

mera!

Motor Drive

F5.6 30mm

Flash off

Flash on

Boots

Compact Camera Outfit with Motor Drive

250MD

200
24 EXP

PROMISE OF SATISFACTION

The prizes

The amazing Boots 250MD camera has every gadget you could want.

The motor drive winds the film on, so you are always ready for the next shot. When the film has finished, the motor will rewind it for you!

There is a built-in auto flash.

It comes complete with case, batteries and 35 mm film. Ready for you to get out and get snapping!

Boots also give a two year guarantee.

Hurry! The closing date for entries is Friday 6 February 1998.

Answers

Pages 18 – 19

Focus on Fruit

1 Apple
2 Kiwi Fruit
3 Peach
4 Orange
5 Banana
6 Pineapple
7 Cherry
8 Strawberry

Cryptic Clothing

 hand wash

 warm iron   wash at 40 °c

 dry clean   do not tumble dry

angora

cashmere

Pages 30 – 31

Green Games

Lemonade bottle
goes down chute A

Jam jar
goes down chute B

Cola can
goes down chute C

Newspaper
goes down chute D

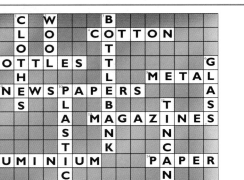

Meaningful words

broken promise

balancing act

 three piece suite (sweet)

 a piece of advice

Puzzle Corner

Quickly
The middle square is the only one to have all sides ripped.